GROUP PORTRAIT FROM HELL

BOOKS BY DAVID SCHLOSS

Group Portrait from Hell
Behind the Eyes
Greatest Hits
Sex Lives of the Poor and Obscure
Legends
The Beloved

GROUP PORTRAIT FROM HELL

DAVID SCHLOSS

CARNEGIE MELLON UNIVERSITY PRESS
PITTSBURGH 2009

ACKNOWLEDGMENTS

I am grateful to the editors of the following publications, in which these poems previously appeared, often in somewhat different form:

The Cincinnati Review: "The Academy Awards;" "At Daybreak;" "The Fourth Stooge; Green Bay;" "I Thought, Yesterday, of Ending It All"

The Columbia Poetry Review: "Appetite;" "The Dakota"

Legends (Chapbook), The Windmill Press, Iowa City, Iowa: "The Myth;" "Portrait of a Man"

Poetry: "The Myth;" "Portrait of a Man"

My appreciation to Kay Sloan, especially, and to Maureen Bloomfield, Jim Cummins, Andrew Osborn, and Jim Reiss, who offered valuable criticism and encouragement as readers of this manuscript-in-progress.

My thanks also to Miami University, and especially to Keith Tuma, for an Assigned Research Appointment, which helped me in the completion of this manuscript, and for financial support in the publication of this book.

Book Design by Chris Monti

The publication of this book is made possible by a grant from the Pennsylvania Council on the Arts.

Library of Congress Control Number 2008923988
ISBN 978-0-88748-498-8

Printed and bound in the United States of America

10 9 8 7 6 5 4 3 2 1

CONTENTS

I. In History

II. In A Dream

III. Inheritance

IV. In Love

for my family and friends,

my teachers and students

"Evil stems from the inability of people
to sit still by themselves inside a room."
—Blaise Pascal, "Pensées"

"Or could Pascal have been not entirely right
about sitting quietly in one's room?"
—Elizabeth Bishop," Questions of Travel"

I. IN HISTORY

"Every luxury has its cost
in someone else's suffering—
and everything's a luxury,
beginning with this world . . ."
—Cesare Pavese

APPETITE

From the first day, we wanted to indulge
our appetites, our visceral yearnings
for more, to taste the quivering jellies

of touch, blood infusing skin with new heat
at the summits of our chests, the moist caves
of our mouths, to crawl into flesh forests

to restore some passage through greenness, sun
flashing in branches snapping before us
as the world hurtled, shadow-splashed, the air

speaking a language only we could hear—
the winds, the whispering networks of nerves,
inside our privacy, a deep clearing

surrounding us kneeling at the entrance
to the waiting, tangible, glistening world.

Adam

The earth seems featureless at first, then clear,
leaves stirring as we watch beneath the moon
flamingo-colored dawn come flaring soon
through azure air, and figures reappear.

Can we divine some patterns from the birds'
wings streaming through the envelope between
our vision and day's difficult new sheen,
to realize God's reasons, flown past words?

Great sacks of winds have captured all the mute
confessions from the darker holds of trees,
unfolding over loam—out where, torn free,
gnarled branches, roiling waters, flood the roots.

Yet, what we shed at night, like shards wave-tossed
along that shore, returning, still retains
some sense of order caught within the strains
of rising winds pressed out to sea and lost—

and such sad music fills us when we feel
we've given up all former visions of
forgiveness for not heeding His hard love
with equanimity, becoming 'real'. . .

Looking farther outward in this strict light,
we, too, feel swept apart, our bodies just
limbs swaying as we tumble like some dust
through air, giving rise to new thoughts of flight.

But why still play at half-forgetting why,
as if each cruelty's no act of will,
our flesh breaks into differences that spill
new blood that spreads, once shed, across the sky?

Is it the fallen world, or sight's dim screen?—
the whole process projected like our dreams,
till nothing but our guilty knowledge gleams,
seeping into and over everything.

Eve

That slim ambassador to this world hissed,
"Remember to maintain your innocence
to Whoever judges you—" and soon I knew
our Judge would surely find us where we kissed
among the other carnal animals . . .

We came to rest outside those gates awhile
in our abandoned days. We fell to earth
because of Pride, I think, and gradually
guilt changed to quiet guile; once-charming smiles
uncomplicated as unopened eyes grew dim.

The sight of genitals that turned our heads
now fills us with disgust. We share the shame
of bargaining for old lives back, and hate
the costs of laboring. That snake had said,
"Lift up your arms, enjoy your dripping skins—"

but, even as we leave old skins behind,
we can't sort out our former freedoms from
new habits, toiling through these mortal lives
because we were prohibited to find
and eat the fruit that hung so ripe before us.

Our passions lost us possibilities,
the world divided into two—just us,
who exercised our wills, and all the rest—
once we desired to know complexities,
as if unwrapping were itself the gift . . .

Amazed how crime can saturate a face,
we've come to bear responsibility
for blasphemy, become our common tongue,
our sad monopoly on sin—disgraced
thieves hanging at the zenith of our grief.

ABEL

A tiller of fields, but not
a herder of sheep or goats;
a keeper of the old tales,

he cultivated such skills,
gazing past full pens and folds
into sheaves of golden light,

until, Cain-struck, he fell
upon his own field of wheat.

THE GENERATIONS

Their gardens planted squarely with designs
against some colder times, the extended family
never expected much better climates for
all they were worth: their wintry need for seed,
still trampling all the flowers in their beds.

If some less tragic figures would never accept
such difficult lives, consider how they found
their daughters made pregnant by marauders,
misbegotten as their own winter flowers
buffeted by storms of their God's devising.

Yet each new illicit birth was welcomed as
a disclosure of some out-of-season leaves
hovering on the horizon, as winters flower
beyond all former transgressions, expectations—
and we keep whistling, as winds will, through our teeth.

We see the ends of Egypt's royal lines
in desert wastes, the sands' deserted towns
like lushness turned to chaos, jungle vines
the Mayans later crawled back through, or, down
the Indus Valley, peoples lost to swords
in mists from Asian steppes. Did they intend—
those hordes of petty potentates and lords—
their words to be redeemed, or names to blend
together in some future age? All gone,
whatever place or principle of praise
they chose to hang their mortal powers on
through siftings of eternal shifting haze:
uncomprehended emptiness, bare rooms,
the stillness of their desecrated tombs.

The true Etruscans, too, are lost to us
because they fell before new Roman might,
and all their hosts of attributes: just dust
beneath the heaps of years. Such ghosts, at night,
still hover over crusted-over earth,
a crumbling rust that troubles trembling bones
that fell upon their foes, yet perished, cursed
to losing what they wanted most. White stones,
these corpses lived with losses—only the wise
knew even momentary paradise—
then spent the short remainders of their lives
in trampling others' less heroic busts:
for, after all, each simple beggar must
return to earth the coin in which he trusts.

Cheops with his projects, Xerxes with his men,
Alexander's progress, gone to ground again;
Christian Europe's darkness after Rome burned out
the lights of Greece: blank statues' eyes of doubt.
Civilizations flourished, and then declined:
in every remnant of those worlds we find
bones bleached by centuries, forgotten bands
of warriors' hands laid on victim's hands
in casual connection, mutual embrace,
decaying face upon decaying face—
as if the basis of the human race
is to build up, tear down, and then, unmanned,
lie down and die within each captive land
as the lion once lay down with the lamb.

"A ROMAN PROSPECT"

17th c., artist unknown

Late summer afternoon: in golden haze,
old men conduct their trades among old stones
that dwarf them; broken columns stand apart
in slanted light; the richest vegetation
hangs down from pillars forty feet in air.

Beyond the precipice of their present tense,
men seem diminished lines of giants fallen
to ragged sellers of cheap beaten wares,
leaning beneath dust motes that filter through
decaying Rome's collapsed magnificence.

The artist's brush trusts in such immensities:
gathering cloaks about themselves as if
they still held wings, these men approach, on knees,
the vanishing points of distant histories,
the memory of some classical perspective.

As they creep towards distant crumbling hovels
all plastered over with their tattered trappings,
dust's everywhere—the golden-ochre dust
keeps blowing down the narrow passageways—
and, over every face, gold leaves its fading trace.

THE FOURTH STOOGE

There once was a fourth, mysterious Stooge,
a favorite of that former *derrière-garde*:
unpaid, he stood in for the rest, off-stage,
a sort of wiped-up asshole to the stars.

He was a bouncing-back-up, wind-up-toy
of a boy, quickly falling to the floor
without complaint, even seeming to enjoy
taking his lumps, then coming back for more.

Behind the scenes he practiced pratfalls, dazed
eyes closed (although he always hit his marks)
or, pie-eyed, caught the custards in the face,
knuckles to the skull, received the hardest knocks.

From that true school of cruelty he took
the unrelenting punishment they dealt
with equanimity: he sometimes shook,
but never mentioned what it was he felt.

We thought he was some proto-anti-Scrooge
who wasn't in it for the money or the fame—
but, unashamed, that perfect Stooge's Stooge
became too good at losing losers' games.

THE AVIATOR

Howard Hughes

Some tried to peel beneath his layers, seeing
the sadness past his charming everyone,
winning at everything, even sleeping
with Hepburn, filming all his other women
in simple simulations of right and wrong,
old movie dreams never leaving him alone.

Becoming used to finding fingerprints
on those many starlets, was he sickened by
a world of germs then, always swarming in?
He'd look around the rooms to see which ripe
bodies were worth the picking—yet he spent
more time in cockpits flying, smoking his pipe.

Up in the air, did he think his destiny
was voices in his head, which always said
there's nothing better he could do than fly?
He didn't want to know what the logic was
for panic attacks, his quarantined dread,
the burdens of compulsions he'd keep from us.

He didn't need to tell the Fourth Estate—
they knew of his affairs, his "air of a god,"
his eating every night the same peas and steak—
but, exposed, supping at those swanky clubs,
in his mind someone always had to pay
for this life, an endless series of hard jobs.

Since engineering was his greatest skill,
the way he'd slip behind another armor,
he made good use of his propulsive will
as mastermind behind the scenes, prime mover,
naming all his driven things—like a god, still—
though the chatter in his head was never over.

He wanted some return to health, to flourish
by flying through rough weather, flying blind,
almost killing himself with each new crash—
until, at last, altogether tightly wired,
sadder than anything he'd ever defined,
sick and tired of everything, he retired.

Lost in Las Vegas, where, in drugged-out sleep,
bad luck cost the poor as much as the rich,
were his inexorable losses worth the trip?
Post-Hollywood, the dreams had never ended,
but hotel holdings held some greater interest:
like his fingernails, they could be extended . . .

Did he hope to make his whole world whole again
inside a place he'd prepared to lie in,
on his own uncertain terms, until the end?
He'd trained himself—it was his fixed idea—
to be commanding, so placed his period
at the end of his sentence, disappeared.

AGAINST THE BOMB

Some spoke of *making love not war,*
but some hard cases held their ground
against new blooming mushroom clouds.

Within this world, haphazard, crazy,
could they beat back what they'd been shown
of hell, using their own hot bodies?

Destruction spread itself out slowly
and, down below, it called their names
to come and meet it—so they came.

At first, they hunkered down and felt
their backs unburdened, even soothed,
upon those sands that seethed with heat.

The earth seemed like a furnace there:
they lay on it with more and more
respect for flames inside its core.

It might cost them everything they knew,
they knew, but they'd risk everything
to try to put an end to suffering:

looking forward to feeling no worse
nor better than the days before,
some talked of clarifying war . . .

WATCHING THE ENDLESS WAR ON TV

Dying flowers in the third person,
disguising intricate skies as hard
bones indicate no sense of suffering

as the pictures flash into the bar
where we are, arguing with others
about the soldiers we see diving

softly into fields, bodies falling
down chutes, growing into grass, until,
being plowed under, yet increasing,

the first person, I think, is only
a survival of some part of speech,
and peace is just a short revival.

Since segregation was coming to an end,
to save their privacy, they gathered stones:
maintaining walls meant everything to them.
Accumulated guilty anger soon
filled all their privileged environments
and ruined the confines of exclusive rooms.

While "Negroes feel we owe them for their years
of servitude," what propped these people up?
On their last legs, they'd fed on racial fears
so long, fear seemed the only uncorrupt
thing left to them—and yet, fear still appeared
a screen through which new holes would soon be cut.

They thought to save an old *noblesse oblige*
to keep their whitewashed histories intact,
projecting new solutions on the streets—
but felt hard-pressed between positions as
they peered at strangers' windows, where they'd meet
their own reflections, noses flat against the glass.

GOLDEN OLDIES

As the doo-wop quartet is singing
its last, the pure falsettos thrilling
the atmosphere, the stagehands raising
curtains of smoke to drift above
the well-kept crowd's rapt contentment,

We tell it, don't sell it, they shout,
no longer that group once cast as
harbingers of hope for the world—
now just misty reminders of
misery in their old neighborhoods.

Straining for air, the crowd can't wait
to rise up with applause that works
a little bit like laughter: it hurts,
yet lightens our lugubrious loads.

THE DAKOTA

At first, I thought it seemed not quite yet dark
enough for lights around the labyrinthine
Dakota, that looming huge apartment building
at the western edge of New York's Central Park.

Like passing the police beside a road
with bleeding victims of fresh accidents
in blankets, waiting for the ambulance,
and speeding on, with someplace else to go,

I didn't think such things could ever happen
where taxis pulled inside to let them out—
but there had been the shots, the blood, then shouts
of *Someone killed John Lennon!* through Manhattan . . .

Subletting for a month, that gray December,
I lived around the corner, not long since
he'd walked out into crowds with vigilance:
they'd celebrate the singer and remember

his dissent as peaceful protest—or indecency—
the real charisma of the superstar
as handsome vagabond—or troubadour
manqué in settled domesticity . . .

They set aside their differences that day:
they needed love, as if that's all they'd need—
unhappy men and women with love beads
and retro granny glasses on display.

They needed love, a swinging pendulum
from life to death that wouldn't ever mar this
parade of burning candles—their catharsis
to feel responsible, to care for him . . .

With growing crowds that filled the streets in silence,
I didn't dare discuss, since he was gone,
the dangers of *the mob* with anyone—
but knew that singing couldn't stop the violence.

With lessened expectations of Apocalypse,
is Death delayed? We can't forget our fears.
Imagine going on for many years
without car bombings: can we co-exist,
in freedom for, and from, God's chosen people?
But isn't that the point of Israel?

Are armed and isolated settlements
an answer? Bad as our words, dead children's flesh
remains in cries of men and women, fresh
as gloating nightmares of bad governments . . .
But daily talk shows rant on now about
how *we're* the ones who want to kill the State!

Preoccupied with lives reduced to wrath,
is ancient wisdom just a curse, or gift?
Uncertain understanding of this world resists
our taking oaths, in minds and bodies both:
bedraggled spirits waiting for some ending
to songs of war, a peace we'll never sing.

CHERNOBYL

As hard as their lives,
the knells for dying
children deep inside,
we hear the sounds of

hell, chemicals turning
heads to yellow cake,
flesh to melting mush,
lakes of melting ice;

and each lie, precise
and glowing, hushes us
to nightmares throwing
off what we can't trust,

seeing between lines,
no longer nonchalant,
learning the names of
all the dead forgotten.

THE ACADEMY AWARDS

We don't need to keep death's heads
on our desks or beside our beds
when we can tune in each year

and see the living former winners
arrayed in each advancing stage
of disbelief at their own decay.

II. IN A DREAM

THE MYTH

When he reopened that great door
for the first time as a young man
with such innocent hopefulness,

not because he was doing it
for the first time or thinking that
it had never been done before,

but just because it had been done
over and yet over again
in the long history of men

and would continue to be done
as he became an older man
with uncertainties he would learn

upon going through other doors
with a sense of this history
projected in his hopeful plan:

to be refreshed anew each time
he reentered that certain myth,
an emblem of an act of faith

that even if that first doorway
is rubble now and the old place
he entered no longer exists

the meaning of that entrance as
a fresh beginning of belief
might keep protecting all his sleep.

At the village pond, "That Old Time Religion"
is a favorite song; young men wake at dawn
to work; and hand-fed swans swim in the sun . . .

When it snows across the roads, they clear them
by 5 a.m., yawning before dawn, because
the school needs it. They need a preacher, too:

once, they shared one with another town;
now, there is none. They sing out, anyway,
with that old time religion, at work, at play,

their favorite tunes—and clear a heavy snow
off the dangerous bridge: it's necessary
to shovel paths across the icy river . . .

And there are other stories, told in profiles,
of people going busily about their tasks;
critiques of *who does what* belies their faith.

One woman calls the genial plumber in
to fix her pipes. It isn't that much work,
but that's the worst she's ever had to face.

Now, she sings in the shower, coloratura,
with plenty of lavatory bravura,
on one cold morning, in the steamy mirror . . .

Outside, to clear a barren field, they burn it,
with wicks soaked in fuel from one man's car.
They say to the one who provides the fire,

With your help we won't need a minister;
since he left you've been our good advisor . . .
Without irony, all earnest and sincere,

their faces tell their stories. Dressed in black,
their characters seem quite convincing as
we leave the theater, singing with their singing.

THE FIRST PLAGUE

God, in his anger, or mercy, would take
every eldest son: we heard how cars spun
out of control on dry and empty roads.

As blood ran cold across the countryside,
between the wintry parsonage and fields,
we circled the decaying, emptied squares

we couldn't inhabit, knew the quiet
of cemeteries, all the dying, in time,
flying like winds into our troubled beds.

With a touch of earth buried deep within
the face of our original designs,
from one chapel, then another, the bells

rang out the cold, absorbing, dissolving
like snow into ice, our one and only life.

THE MYSTERY

He found the mystery revealed within
the mountainsides, crevices in rock:
with only six worms crawling there,
the valleys were all wanting water—

and sleep became a hard negotiation
between the muscles and long bones
which filled the tables of those plains
where rivers of dreams once drained.

Surprised by pilgrimages going past
his backyard fence, diminished from
the old migrations, he heard, beyond,
the wild dogs' howling in the wind.

As night gave way to day,
"You mustn't look in the mirror,
too bruised around the eyes,
nor let others know you're seeing
yourself for the first time
as completely dead while walking
around as if alive,"
the voices said to me in sleep,

the way nature in me
reversed itself, like a statue
carved from the inside out,
and I stood, back to the mirror,
in a death mask, my eyes
staring dark behind it, peering,
crying out at the bruised
world beyond the back of my head:

I remained dead / alive
to the morning light streaming in
through the windows, the blinds
blurring, deepening the shadows
like pixilations past
fences of the living world, where
I seemed, inside my bed
asleep, awake within a dream.

We hardly left the house for days, confined
our wishes to big sticks to strike out with,
to keep ourselves intact behind closed blinds—

but when we had to go to work (we lived
by cleaning up the messes others made,
delivering their goods) we felt confused:

what kept us at such menial tasks, low paid—
was it some sick instinct for being used?
Deep in the nights we tried to find a cause:

on one hand, we were hoping to evolve;
on the other, our nails grew into claws
before each dawn, our problems unresolved . . .

And now, at last, collapsed back onto beds,
deep sleep can't wipe those labors from our heads.

So much depends upon the awkward fathers
watching their little children, behind fences,
jumping up and down in pools of rainwater.

And this may be all they'll ever know of love:
precious little—while, hidden ever after,
lying down again upon their burdened backs,

it takes such a long time to pay off their debts,
even to compute all their losses, defeats,
caught up in the terms of their everyday lives.

Each evening, they come home to the children
jumping up and down or crying out from beds
ringed with red balloons like runaway screams.

IN A DREAM

She finds that she's responsible for
a child, the little girl in her care.
At a street fair, hand in hand, they turn
a corner and see the crowd around
The Greatest Outer Space Attraction,
which looks like a seesaw or a plow,
some sort of long wooden contraption.

At one end sits a large masked woman,
a witch-like-figure with wizened skin
and sagging breasts; and, at the other,
a younger woman, waiting to rise
and levitate, to join the mothers
already flying high in the sky,
hovering cheerfully above her.

Is it the carnival atmosphere,
all those onlookers pushing her there,
that makes her be the next to sit down
and pull the clear plastic mask, carried
by the little pet monkey like a crown,
over her head, and not feel worried,
leaving the child to the care of the crowd?

Soon, she's feeling catapulted fast
towards the constellations, soaring past
all her past sufferings from a host
of childhood desires for the profound.
Letting them go, she skywrites in smoke
against the inky blue background,
white letters to the watchers below.

She smiles down at the old fears, surpassed
former selves, benignly flying back
through the universe, and out to where,
over the horizon, she can see
with the others why people explore:
to discover just how thoroughly
they can find a way to disappear.

RUNAWAYS

Projecting love on them like pets,
he thinks his children loved him once—
yet, rubbing up against thin skins,
he keeps peering past half-shut lids,
still wanting to restore those faces
to semblances of former children's.

Once-wedded fingers, he foresees,
will end in ever greater swellings,
auto-immune-like complications—
yet, he feels an old fury to care
for brains they let be left to rot
in chains, in heads all shorn or shaven.

Electricity shoots from the roots
of their hair, and covers their flesh,
tattooed beneath their tattered clothes,
while, nakedly, heart on his sleeve,
he goes out walking, block to block,
to block out where those lids first closed.

How many others have crawled out
from bedroom windows, broken pulses
blooming in their faces and feet?
Acclimating to their loss, he finds
himself also missing, stripped past
whatever he once could believe.

A LITTLE NIGHT MUSIC

The noise of the radio
tapping into my brain
another busy signal;

the static of the radio
like a firing squad
pulling their triggers:

a tap on my shoulder;
the killer in the mirror;
the pull of the trigger . . .

Outside the window,
having turned to stone,
the killer in the mirror

holds still long enough
to be backed into
by a parked car.

A.A.

Each day, he takes another pledge
never to let himself feel bad
enough to take a drink again.

Since liquefaction's grown within
from all he's drunk and done, he's come
to know how vast that ocean seems:

aquatic mammals, too, may drown—
and he, who knows sobriety
as possessions know possession,

must press his hands together, make
a makeshift prayer at any hint
of hollowness. But he can't tell

if, buoyant, he'll betray himself—
how, as he once plied the squeegee
or played the squeezebox every day,

he still reports the pitfalls in
the process of his drying out,
his constant urge to set things straight.

RUINS

The futures of his heady pasts:
old houses haunted now with ghosts
in brackish waters, crackling glass,

frail bodies bound only to fail—
like puzzles tumbling into pieces,
yet, reassembled in detail,

those nervous shouts of laughter, dread
remaining in the salty wakes
of tears. He takes with him fresh bread

and water for these journeys down
cracked tracks, faint trains of thought that pull
past weed-choked stations, signals gone,

to find some living scenes among
those old tableaux in his good time—
so many other ways gone wrong

or come to grief. . . . And though he's grown
past innocence, at least he's pleased
to know how much he's never known.

PORTRAIT OF A MAN

As his mirrors capture the room in which
he embraces us, they kiss the surfaces
of shining woods with reflections off
his family photographs: his whole life seems
the perfect history, unraveling,
of a child whose outcast look, whose shock
of fine hair, are not yet fugitive
but present in this room where he has been
measured to fit firmly into his future.

Now his eyes are wet with the past, the pall
and clutter of years disengaging some tears
as he sits in a silk robe before us,
freshly laundered and showered and shaved,
having made a pact with his demons
to give himself up, body and soul,
to whatever privacy possesses him—
to be talking quietly in this place
while his eyes follow a path years away.

We're discussing the weather in the west,
monetary restraint, when his look at last
admits his exhaustion—then vanishes,
wandering off to a sunny summer house,
another country, where he relaxes
rearranging the furniture, reliving
some adventure with such bright clarity
that time seems to stop everything for
a man in a silk brocade dressing gown.

And when it's time for ending the evening,
his head bowed before the thought of parting,
the darkness comes in through the windows
without any warning, driving us out
to the elevator dropping to earth,
his voice from above filtering down
like siftings of light at the end of a tunnel,
reflecting only ourselves back to us then—
as he remains, lost to us in the night.

THE WAGES OF AIDS

Without a hope for what he'd hoped to find
        beyond some self defined
by local marriage laws, his being gay,

he's disenchanted with this rougher physics,
        bad coughs becoming drips,
as flesh gives way to gravity, each day . . .

He's feeling little, like a boy again,
        who grew to love a man—
which brings a sense of old romance to bear—

so he's been learning how to temporize
        with voices bound inside
his head, although their purposes appear,

when all his friends now come with handkerchiefs,
        as simply living, riffs
made grave without the love they used to make.

Not giving up, a kind of living will
        for friends who visit still,
he stays brave for his own sweet loving's sake.

HOSPICE

The processes of dying are so common
the final stages seem predictable:
first, there will be the loss of appetite,
uneven shallow breathing, dehydration;
then, rapid swings of body temperature;
finally, agitation, hallucinations . . .

While the faithful family sits and waits
around the hospital bed in her room,
outside the windows clouds tell a story
of evanescence: *Why is there anything*
before it soon goes, lost to posterity. . . ?
And now she's hot, and now she's cooler, still.

Throughout it all, she feels as if she's falling
from a great height, and we can only fight
that panicked feeling with infusions of grief;
because we don't know the comforting words
to help save her from these vertiginous days,
we try by hugging her, keeping her warm.

There always seems to be some undertow
pulling her out to sea, new waves of tears
beneath a cloudy sky we can't wash away—
but we can help her steer her little boat
across those waters where she can complete
her own completion, make it mean something . . .

Before she comes to her own conclusions,
all wisdom seems a confusion of things:
the present becomes much less interesting,
and the vertigo persists. Our questions
have only other questions as their answers—
though we will not forget: she *did* resist.

After all, blood-rivers run through the sewers
on the way back home to the sea, and though
she turns a blind eye, which falls to the floor
as she turns to the wall, she may be thinking
how best to make her wishes known to us
before we return to the rest of our lives.

THE DREAM AS GIFT OF HAPPINESS

Last night, my father came to me in sleep
and said to tell two people of my dreams
so they might come to share their own with me.

As friends converse about their waning days
in passing small details, "I'm going on
a trip," I said, "preparing for some change."

I moved my car, and gave my keys to him
to pile some boxes in, so they would keep.
But once we'd packed and filled it with my things,

a pocket watch lay out beneath the trees:
its hands showed times my cousin John and I
stood taking pictures of our childhood street.

I never thought we'd find ourselves again
like this, on common ground, since, for a time,
we hardly ever spoke at all. . . . And then,

those souls, life-size, no longer standing where
our bodies once were deep in conversation
under golden shade, slowly disappeared.

"It's true, you're with us on the other side,"
my father said. But they'd been dead for years.

III. INHERITANCE

THE WILL

The way some people wait until their lovers
fall fast asleep to tell them of their love,
I'll wait until they're gone to eulogize
my friends, to will them back inside their lives.

When one friend dies, his great unwritten film
encyclopedia will lie lost with him;
when my father died, at least six languages
still languished in his cancer-ridden brain.

After a while, his will got besotted, soaked,
as if too dimmed to get life's bitter joke:
practicing science, we get too few slippery
opportunities to understand this world.

When I go, of course, one exquisitely fine-
tuned set of critical distinctions between
contemporary prosodies—as tortured
as they may seem—will disappear anon.

I come to my own age with willed endurance:
when I consider all the shoplifted goods,
piles of rich food, hoarded words' extravagance,
I fall silent, too, before each lack of grace.

Gray days, my hitchhiking thumb points away,
some will returning to old arrested dreams,
bestowing myself in subconscious forms
as nightmare animals beget their clones:

it's easy to write oneself down with loathing
out of self-love—the vast majority
of literary hopes all too soon betrayed
by calculating boys uselessly employed—

all searching for how best to rewrite their wills.

The unexamined question's not worth asking,
but, in the accidents of my time passing,
what if I arrived each day a little late
for anything to happen, and missed the boat?

A sensitive person may still shrink away
when *love* glides past—to be haunted always
by what remains of merely living: waste,
regret and sadness—poets' themes—like Yeats.

My fantasies are more blue-collar stories:
a small commercial building looms before me
at the corner of two dark and narrow streets,
in a neighborhood I wouldn't be, ordinarily—

but, since I've worked here on a film, recording
and reporting several murders, violent muggings
and a rape, I've seen revenge aesthetics,
avengers with black raincoats, sharp prosthetics.

Then, lawyers would arrive with business cards
to pass out at the spectacles of blood
I can't forget: Life teaches violent ways
to undistinguished men—then goes its way.

It's how you think that makes your world, it says,
barking orders like gangsters from the Forties—
but then, Life's always beating someone up,
or gets the better of the deal, by grin or gun.

And if I risk interpretations now,
it's obvious I'm feeling hunted down
myself, still trying hard to come to terms
with Nothingness and Being, common words.

AN ANTHOLOGY PIECE

As someone reading an old book sometime
may come upon a long-forgotten name,

print might win you another, second chance
to reward an accidental future glance

into moments of feeling beyond your death,
as polished mirrors hold a last breath—

though trying to develop some public skill,
like anything rare, may feel ephemeral

and possibly fading for an unknown reader,
remaining, like you, a private figure.

1. Bird against the Window

Past interfering in human affairs,
his gods are silent relative to breath:
not one cries out with sympathetic fears
for the small amount of change he has left.

So little satisfies a mind that plays
at rendering rich futures, which he reads
himself out of like pictures torn from frames,
he does scant justice to such tapestries.

When he looks down the spectral corridors
where actual and dreamlike mists collide,
each painful future subject still appears
as stillborn, subject to vicissitude.

An ophthalmologist prescribes new glasses:
"Your clouded lenses see in mono-vision,
so can't perceive your life for what it is
beneath the sun, clear, out in the open . . ."

From cowardice or pride, he'd rather not
discuss the stupider mistakes he's made—
until his therapist cries out, "What's that?"
when, fervent bird, he flies against the pane.

"Because I'm such a creature of aesthetics,"
he answers, "must I put myself in danger
of clemency from this world's architects?
I'd rather be, instead, my own true monster."

2. Resurrection

The constantly revivifying myths—
calamities beyond the End of Days,
lost Edens, our eternal lives and deaths—
cleanse his attention in new paraphrase.

How feasible is it to suffer things
before he takes a logarithmic leap
past helpless unreflective sufferings
to *logos,* rhythmic words with which to keep

flesh coming back to him in new rebirth?
He recreates some welcome space around
a consciousness of self upon the earth,
a self emerging from the common ground—

and spends his time now flying all about
with thoughts of worlds composed of castoff souls
and dying bodies raised inside and out
of primal earthen elements. Wormholes

through dirt are dumbly filling up like plates,
reflecting what he'll have to go without
for all his failing myths which mediate
no honest Paradise transcending doubt.

With cancerous brain, he dismembers gods
as dying ideas he can't reconceive
from old inscriptions of the human odds,
errant, thinking, *"Only some shall still believe."*

Of my urge to fly
my paraplegic teacher
seems to be quite proud.

Though no one's going
to bow or scrape or kowtow
to him anymore—

not me, at least, no
longer afraid of the truth
in his fateful form:

on the surface he's
a still pool, blurring into
conflicting ripples . . .

Since he no longer
gets his hands into his wife's
cups, he's in his own:

"Bashō's another
sodden poet who often
fell out of his boat."

"Oh, no, it was that
other drunk Chinese guy who
first swallowed the moon."

AN EVOLUTION

The form that history takes:
it's our flesh rising up next
to dance, newly inhabiting
the antique shapes that keep
a sense of past orders intact.

As evidence of their beauty,
minds make their own style
of thought, the most cogent
collecting in a wind's wake
flying crumbs, bones' debris.

So we may claim the bounty,
who waited so long as limbs
sprang back up in our faces,
striking us in arcs of rising,
we think we'll climb forever

into the earth's soft cocoon,
each word a darkened haven
from all the language inside
our heads, slowly compiling
some music from the moles.

If taking possession of this
world of wonders moves us
like triumphal music, scores
alluding to scenes of saving
grace for the recently raised,

embracing our complexities,
even shaking, swimming in
and out of deepening waters,
forsaking an acceptance of
what simply is isn't so hard:

other kinds of consciousness
fade, finally, out of energy,
it seems, so there's nothing
left to say for us, as long as
this dance to Nothing lasts.

"HOW CAN YOU STAND IT, BEING OLD?"

Why do some young people
turn into such old cripples,
constantly moaning over
the minutiae of their decay?

They bitch about their skins
thinning, peeling like paper
from walls, which also fall
and flail against the winds.

Sun-punched in our faces,
we moved into new places,
soon started watching out
for some winding way back.

While others cry out above
increasing static and noise
from the playing of radios,
the bumps on numb roads,

we'll hear the loud reports
of busses on the highways,
where life feeds on old life
and straight lines converge.

AN UNDERSTANDING

Of gods as useful metaphors—

As the stars start to stir, repeating
themselves endlessly, pitilessly,
how could he think he might attain,
even achieving some great age,
a new understanding—like ghosts
of something more to be seen when
coming around to the other side?

Before he came to disbelief
in the heavens as consolations,
he misread the gods' archaic notions
of their mock-serious intentions
for so many years; at each course
of fresh waters falling, his figure
was flooded with less than success.

Had he become the infidel
they made of him because he thought
he was liable to stand up
to what those hidden forces in
the clouds let fall from chariots?
If ever asked, "*Where* are *those carts*?"
"*Before your horses*," he'd reply.

Such fantasies lighten his step,
but, as clods of clay cannot rise,
yearning for something greater yet
to come forth, unforced, from the skies,
unsatisfied, now he shouts out
to the clouds, calls them down as rain
in answer to his own earthly names.

INHERITANCE

It's the light, the light
of suns first forming,
igniting at their cores

a greater movement
of elements evolving
into earthly gravel,

gritty matter beneath
our feet, standing by
water, grimly waiting

to pay a price for all
this world's luxuries.
The reason? Reason:

the way this world
moves in metaphors
inside of our minds,

as if *a love of depths*
means *fear of success,*
ideas flowering from

wetness, like bloody
afterbirths flung back
to the stars, patiently

burning to expire, yet
still shining like coins
inside our palms from

long ago. So, we add
some slain adventurers
of the head and hands

to more recently dead
men and women who
made riffs of voices,

the gifts they left us,
our thanks done, gone.
But the urge to grow

grows, like silent film
explosions, slowed by
rough plaster, caught

within the molds of
thick walls closing in.
Soon, our chest flesh

stands up, gives off
new heat, like nectar
spreading thicker in

an overflow of stress:
"Like lava," we think,
still straining to find

some kind of purchase
on the earth, the heart-
rending fact that it is.

ONE MAN'S BURDEN

He's like a solitary monk who's pleased
to receive some worldly representatives
who seek to find in him a saving grace—

but he's also one, quixotically engaged,
who finds himself more commonly alone,
the burdens of his energies released

by all those other distant hurtling bodies
that push his flesh out to the edge of space,
where he's like a star, without apologies

for self-regard, whose light, chimerical,
suggests he's lived with gravity too long;
a solemn still life, slowly decomposing,

(the rotting meat, bowl of blackened fruit),
so we can see how certain things collapse—
but it's the hair shirt that saves him at last,

the one that he gives us off of his back.

POST-MORTEM

We always thought there was a world beneath
this one, but told ourselves consoling lies,
not worrying about the sharper teeth
that chew the flesh. So, laughing past each threat,
yet helpless to resist the sunset skies,
we traveled towards death's darker maw, its throat.

Our churning arms just served to urge us on
to those last meals, exposing bones inside
the future tense from which no one returns
once they've been introduced to slow decay,
the dominating forces that reside
in soil: they rotate all our crops, don't they?

Though we once thought ours weren't mortal acts
before those last catastrophes—like dreams
converging on bad ends before the facts—
we couldn't save ourselves from acid rains,
or cut the crap before it seeped to streams,
and buried things came crawling out again.

Now we only know earth's crust, its mystery:
how big feasts come from little recipes.

GROUP PORTRAIT FROM HELL

The mouths with missing teeth mere holes
into greater cavities, their souls
through world-corrupted faces stare

beyond the viewer, towards the grave
conceptions that await them where
there's nothing, nothing left to save.

But do we need them to apprise
us of the need to lead lives differently?
Beyond such self-abasement, eyes

that yearn for touch incessantly,
we see each hand that reaches for
the next cannot connect, estranged—

until we come to that far shore
where burning leaves the pain unchanged.

will be complicated, we understand:
as if captured in the beaks of huge birds
flying back and forth attached to taut wires,
we'll create a complex network of sounds.

As if captured in the beaks of huge birds,
in the reconciliations of our cries
we'll create a complex network of sounds
beyond our soon-to-be-vacated rooms.

In the reconciliations of our cries,
the notes that echo others in their chords
beyond our soon-to-be-vacated rooms,
their meanings will not be about solace.

The notes that echo others in their chords
will be complicated: we understand
their meanings will not be about solace,
flying back and forth attached to taut wires.

Today was a good day:
I read a good book
to find out how to
resolve my mysteries.

"The future's enforced
beyond its messengers—
so save yourself," it said,
"before it's too late:

even if you don't like
what it does to you
when He doesn't do good
enough things for you,

God knows, if you won't
get ready for Him
yourself, He'll have to get
ready for you instead."

I THOUGHT, YESTERDAY, OF ENDING IT ALL

"I'd like to get it over with, let my teeth
rot out, cut my hair to the roots, or shave
it all before I go completely bald—"
a friend once put it to me as I trimmed
his hair, thick fingers full of thinning strands

falling to the floor. Now, nothing returns
to fullness, but some pleasure still remains
from the fingering, the shaping, the feeling
of closeness for the time it took to cut
that intimacy of shared fallings away.

Is life no longer worth living because,
thickened by middle age, it moves so slowly
towards final decline? All that will happen
in its own good time, I suppose, but why
hasten the ending when an arm still hangs

from its socket, runs down along my side,
though with consequent pain in the shoulder?
Once, it lifted like a tonearm rising in
the air to end a record's playing, or,
one lover rolling off another to sleep.

IV. IN LOVE

IN LOVE

In our never-ending yearning for
the other, the object of each search,

hands try to clasp what we can't ever
quite grasp, burning beyond like a torch

or candle set before us, which shines
a light behind our eyes, in our minds.

Being burned turns us back to ourselves,
but, turning aside, backs to the world,

love's dying means, *at least, we once lived,*
as just living seems *already dead . . .*

So we'll make love, if that's what it takes
to resurrect all the old mistakes.

ROAD PAVED WITH GOOD INTENTIONS

We always struggled to achieve
the ultimate in politesse,
and made some glum apologies
to keep a calm connectedness.

Resisting inconsistencies
in combinations of the flesh,
we celebrated niceties,
defining needs as neediness.

But interpreting all incidents
in terms of manners didn't stop
destructions of the innocents:
becoming like corrupted cops,

we wrote citations every day,
yet let the real offenders get away.

COOLNESS

He holds her awhile,
wrapped in a blanket,
like a bread basket

on a warm table.
Soon the heat begins
to spread, and opens,

encompassing dreams
of other times, loves,
with memories of

fallen fruit that seems
no more hollow than
fruit upon the stem.

But he doesn't mind
her turning away
when he turns away:

they've long since declined
desires to be kind
to their own sad kind

appearing within
this chilling yet still
lurid carnival.

LISTENING TO THEIR JAZZ

The dissonance musicians make
when arguing against each other
filters through the windows, shakes
dividing air like reckless thunder.

There's the electricity of sex,
expensive, cheap, the old perfumes
of fear, in which we sense what's next
for us inside these noisy rooms.

Before we give out all our sparks
and try some desperate getaways,
a close strike leaves us in the dark,
surrounding us with smoky haze;

then, like the lights that lightning takes,
the storm dissolves us in its wake.

ON HIS DEAFNESS

He can't hear what she means to say,
but walks away, unwitting of
the deep expressions of her love—

just background noise, reduced to gray
that covers him in overweening
ignoring of her needs—too dense,

oblivious, without the sense
to understand the many meanings
of that high music he can't hear,

her rising frequencies of fear
decaying, like his need to know
where senses go to when they go.

"Now we know," I say,
"how not to be happy,"
remembering mainly
how blue sky, by day,
will fade out the stars.

Yes, even early things
will go and stay away
in our perfection of
doing almost nothing,
staring into space.

"Unsatisfied," you say,
"to remain unsatisfied,
our hearts, in secret,
return to a place where
we once used to play."

Over the long haul,
we'll have seen it all:
a cockroach on a wall
can't fly, so tries to
reason before heaven.

The longer we live
the more things become
irretrievably broken:
"I am your nemesis,"
I say, "you are mine."

Although we play at
independence, our own
ideas now seem farther
away, we're afraid,
from ever being born.

"We know nothing willed
will ever yield a world,"
you say, "though we're bent
on smoothing the waves
out of all the oceans . . ."

Cowardly, you'd think
we might become loathe
to stay this way, yet
we continue to dance
our inertial ballet.

UNREPENTANT NEW YEAR'S RESOLUTIONS

First, I'll cut loose—but, think of all the squalls
I'll have to face, the fraught confessions, tears,
my eyes becoming like some abject animal's
while rearranging calendars from former years.

I'll take a stand, admit what I may soon regret—
the shouts, the howls, the snarls—regurgitate
an endless loop of words: *too old, too fat,* a threat
Security will catch, and watch it, caught on tape.

In these new heart-bypassing operations—
I've even planned for unplanned flooding then—
I'll float through tearful reinterpretations,
returning to some new beginnings once again.

He thought she was "a girl with a crush," who'd rather
fantasize about their affair than ever really be together:
such was his indifference, even to his worst behavior,
when he propositioned their old best friends' daughter
and all this came out, running like contaminated water,
laundered through the sewage system of their suburbia.

It was at about this time when he first began to realize
that his wife was not like his mistress—who was liable
to be auctioned off to somebody else; therefore, liable
not to make trouble—but more like a child, or actress,
who'd make a scene and spill her guts for an audience
soon after someone abandoned her for somebody else.

As for his wife: she left vegetables in the refrigerator
when she left him, but took all the meat in the freezer
and left no note when she moved out. It was like war,
World War III, she thought, and tried to run for cover:
bombs were already being dropped, she'd discovered,
threatening civilization as she knew it, sadly, forever.

Their subterranean warfare was revealed to all at last,
like tanks sitting on the front lawn—as overt as that—
and, out in the open, everything was blowing up, fast.
As the neighborhood's news traveled quickly, passed,
knowledge of his character began festering inside her:
Why hadn't she seen this coming sooner? they asked.

At the first reunion meeting she set up between them,
Old Unreliable was his usual self, thirty minutes late;
almost didn't even make it; had to break another date—
with *her*, she assumed, as she sat, smoked and fumed—
forgot the papers; stayed fifteen minutes; "had to run."
Yet, her exasperation became a kind of colder comfort:

his antagonistic sense of unconcern seemed no different
from what she'd lately gotten used to feeling about him,
their two kids, herself, the failed marriage, living alone—
the devil-may-care attitude of one who never even cares
enough to try to hide it. And this, strangely, sustained her,
when it might have warned of her own destructive nature.

"Where's that damned piece of blue-and-white china?"
she said, looking through boxes with her own new lover,
a dark, quiet gentleman with a charming, gentle manner,
while chagrined, past the charm, at *his* lack of concern—
unlike her husband, a man who, whenever he was home,
was always ready to get angry, to fight, slash and burn.

It was at about this time when she first began to realize
this new man's voice was also distant, thin, and sappy,
and, when she was with him, she wasn't all that happy.
She looked at the unpacked boxes and felt like a lover
who'd rather play at marriage than go through it, ever,
counting on men, for years, to keep her always angry . . .

It was at about this same time that he began to realize
that, alone, he was lonely: he couldn't live without her.
So he called her up, acted contrite, and asked his wife
(now ex-wife) if, sometime, they could "get together."
At first, she felt like an actress, playing out the scene;
then, a child again, waking from some terrible dream.

She needed reassurance, and he wanted the insurance
of a nice home life in the suburbs with a faithful wife.
Though their past still cut through them like a knife,
they conducted themselves rather well, considering,
once they'd moved together to another part of town—
and soon led exemplary lives: they had settled, down.

AN ASCETIC'S AESTHETICS

We seek anesthetics for each private
sacrifice of heat: while we want love,
the body's burning, burning alive, it
becomes what we're most fearful of.

Making these weak attempts at peace
with darker figures of desire, instead
of some self-dismemberment, release,
we'll cling to nothing, inside our bed.

We think it's sin within which brings
such throbbing to our skins, so work
to keep ourselves beyond wet dreams
of filmy worlds where lust may lurk.

Yet, when we sleep, a flimsy veil's
thrown over the limits of our days:
like thorn-trees, full of fleshy nails,
each night we scrape ourselves away.

Our vision's to hook up with eager others met
upon a screen, uncovering new worlds, exposed
projections for the eye to buy, becoming bold
as prophets making profits off the internet.

We purchase what we hope may save us, in the sense
that many try to reinvent some thrilling dance
against millenniums of any old romance,
and take positions against the flesh's evidence:

while sharing buttocks, hips, the curly little nests
that shelter shyly hanging things—the clitoris
and inner lips analogous to penises
and scrotal sacs—unhidden parts between their legs,

each human animal seems more or less alike;
amazing how the DNA runs so true to form,
as every nippled breast eventually has come
to differ merely in their final shape and size.

And since each spot-lit crotch we revel in reveals
the fruit forbidden once, its sweetness overlaid
by dangling, dribbling men and women unafraid
to make their livings making love, this flesh won't heal.

But, seeming differences leave some, at least, redeemed:
the flesh, enamored of by those who look no higher
for what romantic human hearts must most desire,
remains attached to simple variations on a theme.

GREEN BAY

He was supposed to be paying
child support, but came through only
the day he won the lottery

in full, the moon each night straying
even in her bed, making war
with the bedclothes—and afterwards,

the little man in the boat seemed
a nubbin guardian, the seat
of old feeling, like an anchor

resting out of wind on the sands,
her latent widowhood exposed
in the shallows of a green bay.

The world seems essentially quiet,
especially on those fine holidays
when our words feel most at play:
behind the workings of tongues
lies silence; behind the workings
of silence lie those same tongues.

Our tongues are tunneling then
into brains, which funnel them,
words draining into the ground—
yet earth's thin skin is no veneer,
but saves the true depth of things,
molecules dancing in its designs.

Design, design: this mad desire
for order almost masks what lies
above or below dividing lines:
with the consequences of flesh
cleft apart, we can barely flesh
each other out, out of our sight.

Now we're hungry for a hunger
that might fill us back up with
some distraction from that hunger
when the unknown appears to us
as what might be made known
through those as yet unknown.

Or, is this just another case of
melancholy, yielding to strangers
whatever a stranger may yield,
as the painted face in a portrait
becomes the face of the painter
reflected in each face he paints?

Soon, as if our joys might tell
themselves behind an open door
and live inside an empty room,
emptiness empties emptiness,
which spreads to fill the space
we will only empty out again . . .

As for our suffering, its limits
seem only the limits of those
who suffer it to live in them,
that sleep that always finds us
when we most want to slip from
beneath the sleep of mere living.

Before such mirrors some actors
enact again within themselves
the art of forgetting themselves:
on stage, voices start to shout—
but it's only one stage towards
forgetting the limits of stages.

For now, the past lies like a dog
on permanent display, stretched
out on a rug, running in its sleep;
while the future is just an idea—
which always pulls out the rugs
stretching out from our ideas.

Keeping some balance means
negotiating between our desire
to rise and an old desire to fall:
entering each other's darkness,
will we bow to the inevitable,
or will it inevitably bow to us?

If the entrances to our bodies
are like caves, and the entrance
to each cave is yet another cave,
will love become like a lamp
flickering in the darkness that
guides the hand that holds it?

While there's still a choice of
punishments—your naked face
before me, or your face not—
now all I want is you to come
back to, to come back to myself,
pervading quiet past the quietude.

DEAR HEART

For all the years
you served me well

by telling truly
how I'd fall

in love, of love's
diminishments,

and always ticked
away my time

with liquid
regularity—

because I don't
expect to die

of cancer like
my relatives,

and since you run
so true to form,

I think that I
will die of you.